WHERE DID THEY COME FROM?
WHERE DID THEY GO?

by Scott Gillam

Editorial Offices: Glenview, Illinois • Parsippany, New Jersey • New York, New York

Sales Offices: Needham, Massachusetts • Duluth, Georgia • Glenview, Illinois
Coppell, Texas • Sacramento, California • Mesa, Arizona

Where did the early Americans come from?

Scientists have long been trying to figure out who the early Americans were and where they came from. We know that the earliest people in North America were hunters because they left their marks on the bones of the animals they killed. These early hunters depended on animals for food. They also used the hides of larger animals for shelter. Scientists believe that during the last Ice Age, what is now Alaska was connected by land to what is now Russia by the Bering Land Bridge. Many scientists formed a theory and concluded that the first people to enter North America were hunters following wild animals across Beringia, sometimes called the Bering Land Bridge.

The Clovis People

Did all the early people who entered North America move across Beringia? Until recently, many scientists thought so. They had found spear points about 13,500 years old near Clovis, New Mexico. These spear points were similar to those found in many other parts of North America. Scientists knew that people had existed in Siberia during the last Ice Age. Scientists believe these northern Asians reached North America across the land bridge. It seemed reasonable to conclude that the Clovis people were descended from northern Asians from Siberia, and that these northern Asians were the first people to come to North America.

Clovis spear points were attached to wooden spears.

The Olmec Culture

The Olmec civilization developed more than three thousand years ago on the plains along the Gulf Coast of Mexico. Perhaps best known for their giant sculptures and massive public architecture, the Olmec show many signs of being Mayan ancestors. The Olmec center was located just west of the Yucatan Peninsula. Like the Olmec, the Maya also used **aqueducts**, had a written language and a calendar. Like the Olmec, the Maya designed their buildings to pay tribute to their gods.

This Olmec figurine of a baby has facial features that are like those of the peoples of Southeast Asia.

4

Mayan bark-paper books contained information for Maya priests, such as material on predicting the future.

The Flowering of the Maya

By about 600 B.C. the Maya were settled in many communities. Some of these settlements would later become large cities. Mayan cities often formed **alliances** with other Mayan cities. The Maya shared many religious and cultural traits.

The Maya recorded their own history using a type of picture writing called glyphics. These were found on stone carvings, kings' tombs, and in a form of a book called a **codex**. In such a book the Maya kept careful trading records, works of literature, science, and history. The Mayan calendar, astronomical figures, and method of writing on bark paper suggest great development.

The Maya began to abandon many of their cities about A.D. 900. What became of the Mayan civilization? There is no single answer to this question. There was conflict between neighboring cities in the Maya Empire and among the different social classes. Growing populations also stripped the rain forest and were very dependent on a weak water supply. Famine, disease, and invasion would have also decreased the population. Together, two or more of these developments likely led to the end of the Maya Empire.

The Aztecs

Just as the Maya were declining in power, another great civilization was beginning. Having migrated from the north, the Aztecs eventually settled in Tenochtitlan (te-noch-tee-TLAHN), which became the capital of the Aztec Empire. On that spot the Aztecs built a city made up of islands called **chinampas** (chin-AHM-phahz) connected by **causeways**. In less than a century, the Aztecs formed alliances and eventually created an empire of perhaps five million people.

Despite the Aztecs' strength, it took the Spanish under Hernando Cortés fewer than two years to defeat them. The end came in August 1521, after a three-month Spanish siege of Tenochtitlan. The Aztecs had no defenses against the siege and the Spanish weapons. After the fall of the Aztec capital, Cortés continued his conquest of Mexico. By late 1521 he was governor of the Spanish colony called New Spain.

Skulls were often used
in Aztec art.

The Fall of the Moche Empire

The early settlers of the coastal area that is now part of Peru may have come from Central America. Around A.D. 100 Moche (MOH-cheh), or Mochica, communities united to form the earliest empire in the Americas. Over the next several hundred years, the Moche developed into a population of at least 100,000. They were known as artistic people. The Moche survived in a dry environment by irrigating their fields with river water and fishing the coastal waters. Like the Inca who came after them, the Moche were led by priests, who wielded a great deal of authority.

Moche pots showed the social level or occupation of a person, shown here by the type of clothing and the decorations.

Moche pots have very realistic designs that can help us learn much about the Moche culture.

The Moche lived in a coastal desert area. Because of this, the area went through periods of drought followed by heavy rain. The rains were caused by El Niño, a weather pattern that regularly brings warm water to Peru's coast. This pattern causes heavy rainfall, which causes flooding. These floods probably washed away much of the topsoil on which Moche farms depended. At the same time, strong offshore winds would have blown sand from the coastal beaches over the fields. That made it even more difficult to grow crops and forced the Moche to move north along the coast. El Niño events also do great harm to any people who rely heavily on the fishing coastal waters, because the water becomes much warmer and fish die. These are some of the reasons the Moche had disappeared by about A.D. 800.

How the Inca Empire Began and Ended

The Inca Empire began between A.D. 1100 and 1200. This empire eventually grew to equal the land area of Western Europe. The first major city of the Incan Empire was Cusco in Peru. Cusco is approximately 200 miles northwest of Lake Titicaca. The Inca did not write. We know something about Inca history from information that has been recorded on **quipus** (KEE-pooz). A quipu is a knotted cord used to keep information. Our knowledge about the Inca still has many gaps.

The Inca Empire was defeated by Francisco Pizarro (fran-SEES-koh pee-SAHR-roh) and the Spanish in 1532. The smallpox that the Spanish had brought with them had already killed millions of Native Americans. Then one of the Incan kings died of the disease. Pizarro arrived during the civil war among the Inca that followed. Through deceit, he managed to defeat both sides without a major battle.

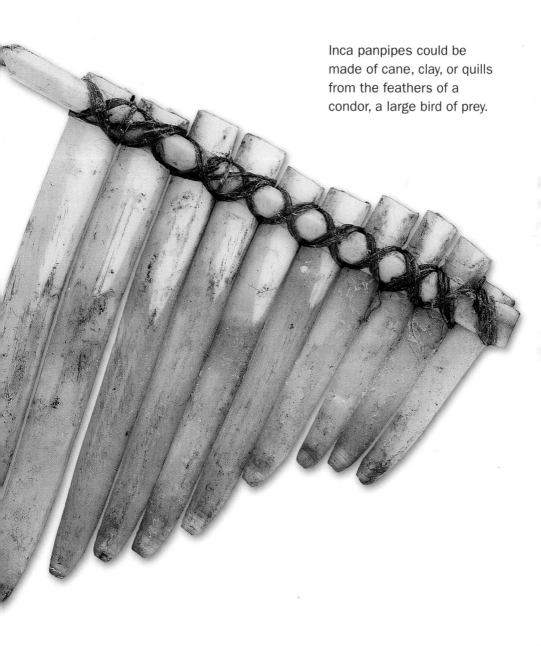

Inca panpipes could be made of cane, clay, or quills from the feathers of a condor, a large bird of prey.

The Anasazi: Pueblo Peoples of the Southwest

The remains of Anasazi (ah-nuh-SAH-zee) **pit houses** and **pueblos** built of sandstone and **adobe** can still be found in the southwestern United States. Though small and isolated, the many Anasazi communities once covered an area the size of South Carolina. The Anasazi may have first come from a group called the Mogollon (moh-GOH-yohn) that once lived in the same area.

There are several possible reasons why the Anasazi suddenly left their homes in the late 1200s. Drought or a sudden change in climate or weather may have kept the Anasazi from growing food. Perhaps an increase in population led to conflict over land and water.

The descendants of the Anasazi still live in the same area of the United States.

So Where *Did* They Come From?

The Aztec are thought to have come from northern Mexico. The Moche may have started in Central America. The Inca probably began in Peru, while the Anasazi are said to have lived in what is now the southwestern United States. Each one of these cultures developed somewhat separately from the others, and each has characteristics that are different from the others. The Anasazi were a peaceful people who believed it was possible to live in harmony with nature. The Aztec, on the other hand, made war on their neighbors and practiced widespread human sacrifice.

Recent discoveries by scientists may provide evidence to support the idea that people in the Americas may have come from two or more places. The 9,000-year-old Kennewick Man was found in 1996 in Washington State. Scientists are still trying to learn about Kennewick Man and where he came from.

Glossary

adobe building material made of mud and straw that is dried in the sun

alliance an agreement made between two or more groups or nations

aqueduct a structure used to carry flowing water from a distance.

causeway a raised bridge made of land

chinampa a man-made island

codex a folding-screen book containing information about predicting the future and religious rituals

pit house a made from digging a hole in the ground and covering it with logs

pueblo a structure of adobe brick

quipu a knotted rope used by the Inca to keep records